For [illegible]

[illegible], [illegible]

[illegible] and [illegible]

[illegible]

# Time of Singing

By
Katharine Wool Parrish

This book is dedicated to John Yong,
our first Korean son,
Who brought with him God's gift of joy
And left us with His peace.

# Acknowledgments

My deep and profuse thanks go to Wendy Parnell, who administered the patterning and publication of this little volume, and to Colleen Parrish whose artistic talents lend beauty and clarity to the poetry of life and this book in particular.

# TABLE OF CONTENTS

## Songs of the Seasons

# Songs of Family

## Songs of Devotion



## Nonsense Songs

# Songs of the Seasons

# Autumn Sky

Stretched-out blue horizon,
Wide, ruff-edged clouds like
Glaciers riding, white and cold
Promises at dawn.

Changing, moving in undulating dance,
The sun-rimmed pillars
Move in imperceptible rhythm,
Dream-dance of departed souls.

Shocking, wildly splashing
Gold, crimson, orange-strewn
Streaming crown of setting sun
On half a world.

Silver spark in a purpling sky,
The mounting orb glows gold
Invitation to celebration
Under a harvest moon.

# Backyard Wonderland

Soft wisps of down twirl and fall
Outside my window.
The porch is crystal-carpeted,
Cozy white cushions fill the swing.
Bare ground spreads a snowy table,
Beneath the birdbath's tiny rink.

Birds brighten the half-light of afternoon,
Black-coated chickadees,
The fat brown wren,
And purple finches fussing at the feeder.
A downy pecks the suet cake,
Cardinals flash across the blank expanse,
Haughty robins search the ground for seed.

I walk the quiet, enchanted lane—
Alone in a silent world.
The trees cotton-tufted, buds wrapped snug,
Brave blades of jonquils, anxious now,
And springtime-colored crocus
Poke through their frigid blanket.

Squirrels scurry to treetop homes,
Grey geese lace their footsteps on the lawn,
Rabbits somewhere secure in holes
Sleep warm while I shiver to discover
This wonderland, this winter whisper
Of a Creator's mind-numbing beauty.

# Dedication

Late spring sunshine warms my back,
Lacy whiteness by the road heralds
Fat, black berries to come.
A bird biting a scrap of string hurries to nest.

Heavy buds burst into leaves that
Cast figured shade on soft new green,
And dusty bulbs fulfill their autumn promise
In rainbow brightness by the porch.

My little one trails his pull-toy
Through the grass and stoops
To hold soft conversation
With the ants who live there.

We walk in the quiet lane,
Speaking of the One Who made him,
And kneel to worship at the cluster
Of dainty violets under a great oak.

*Oh Lord, I pray*
*You'll make his growing-up good,*
*And keep him close to You as he is today,*
*In this four-year-old fellowship.*

# Haiku

I

Dancing springtime rain

Shimmering, splashing sunlight

Silver pearls on green.

II

God of surf and sky

Triumph of the roaring deep

Fill my heart with peace.

# Intricate

Splash, you waves,
In twilight dancing,
Flinging stardust on the sand.

Stand, you mountains
Dark and brooding,
Guardian tow'rs across the land.

Shine, you rivers
Rushing boldly,
Laughing streams and glaciers bland.

Sway, you hemlocks
Reaching upward,
Aeons in your rings are planned.

Sing, you dawnings,
Rose-splashed sunsets,
Marking off the days of man.

Intricate
The whole creation,
Work of an Almighty Hand.

# *Morning Walk*

Spangle-splendored on a fragile web in my path,
Sparkle-tipping each slender needle's green,
Sapphire droplets outline every leaf.
Succumbing to the temptation, I reach up and tug,
Shower the bounty of last night's rain.

# October Beach

The sand, on the sunny side of the dune,
Feels warm to my feet
The morning sky is hung with pastel lace,
A white moon lingers while he can.

I wade in water tingly-cold
And feel a feathery caress—
The auburn tresses of some deep-sea goddess
Brought in to dry on the clean-swept beach.

Offshore, tiny white fishing boats
Pin the ocean's dark and rumpled
Horizon to the hazy blue
Curtain of sky.

# Old Reedy Creek Road

The summer smells are here,
For traveling slow
And cherishing.
Some crisp and sweet; some spicy-dry
At the cooling end of day.

The once-used trail
Leads to tossed old timbers
Softened now with honeysuckle,
Where home was smells of cooking meat,
And apples drying in the rafters.

The road comes creekside,
Catches from above
The Christmas scent of pine,
And winter merriment
On a breeze called memory.

Atop a hill, wild grain can blow
Toasting in the sun,
Dry nutty wisps of bran
On golden heads that nod.

Alone, against a battered, paint-scarred wall,
Glows scarlet in the shabby lawn
One full-descended gladiola,
Remembering.

# O Nata Lux de Lumina

Thou Newborn Savior, Light of Light

O Nata Lux, de Lumina
Sunlight sparkles crystal rivers
Plunging through ice-bound pillars,
Roaring power beneath
The frozen mass of waterfall.

O Nata Lux, de Lumina
Our dark and dingy world
Is clothed in this new, snowy gown;
The hemlocks bow in lacey white
And hillsides roll out calm and clean.

O Nata Lux, de Lumina
Embroidered streams of dotted snow,
Giant icicles formed in weeks of cold
Trap the mountain's stream
Like glistening giants by the road.

O Nata Lux, de Lumina
Thou Newborn Savior, Light of Light,
Whose Heart of Wonder made the worlds,
Touch mercifully our frozen hearts
With the blinding brilliance of Thy Love.

# One Bright Glimpse

I walk the brown October woods
And crunch along the path,
My sad eyes bent on dreariness,
They catch the dusky form
Of fallen oak and dying maple leaves,
And weep.

A sweet bird's call arrests my thoughts.
Through dazzled sun-filled limbs I glimpse
The majesty of wind-shattered light—
Gold on crimson
Orange on green
Amber dancing through.

No longer can I stand and look,
My knees sink to the brown earth-floor,
Beneath dancing hardwood brilliance
And deep-green stalwart hemlock,
In light-encrusted joy
My soul can pray.

# Thanksgiving

The dusty field, fallow after summer's crop
Of soybeans, corn, and watermelon,
Dances in the richness of abundant goldenrod,
Catching and holding the slanting October sun.

Independent maples splash orange-yellow
At the edge of a deep-green wood,
The bashful dogwood sighs blood-red
And willowy by the quiet lane.

The promise of autumn speaks peace,
Quiet afternoons—bright and chill—
Clear evenings, when limbs are bare
And sparkled skies sing unheard harmony.

The gathering of fruit and nuts,
Of firewood and butchered meat,
Brings family and neighbor
Seeking shelter, acceptance and care.

By a fireside where prayers are said,
And tales of generations overlap,
Busy needles click to hum and bump
Of rocking chair and laughter.

Protected from distant wandering,
From hunger, cold, and loneliness,
Inside a house of logs and faith
We come again to thanksgiving.

# Time of Singing

Thoughts on Song of Solomon 2:12
Spring, 2006

The vibrant pod, the tight-closed bud,
The stony sleeping bulb—
In spite of winter's fiercest blast,
Grow still in earth's dark den.

The warmth of April brings release,
The shoving-forth of life.
No branch or grimy plot escapes
The color-splash of spring.

So Christ has burst upon our world
Through sorrow, death and pain.
Released from darkened prophet's lore
On April's bursting Day.

Thou Risen Christ, First Fruit of living spring,
Awaken me to Calvary's loss,
Dawn's victory at an open grave,
Eternal promise, blood-bought majesty.

# Winter Matins

The fiery winter sunrise,
Splashes crimson-gold across
Soft-banked clouds,
Blinding as mountains of diamonds,
Quadrillions of stars together.

Black-lace barren trees
Reach up with fragile fingers.
To greet the silent, frost-filmed day.
Unseen, a mourning dove haunts
The fleeting edge of night.

I bow in wonder, eyes and heart
Now blinded by the glory,
And whisper humble thanks
For the gift of new mercies,
The promise of beginnings.

# Winter Sunset

The eastern sky glows salmon,
Reflecting orange fire
From an out-of-control sunset.

Clouds pulled thin across a clean blue sky
Soften into baby-pink puffs
Brushed by spidery black treetops.

Flaming. . . shifting. . . changing light
Suffuses my universe
And settles on my soul.

Reflected in the lake's smooth face,
Glory turns to quiet dusk
And promises of peace.

# Christmas Spice

Potpourri boiling in its china pot
And spicy cider on the stove.

The trace of pine from the glittering tree,
And cedar logs popping in the fire.

Turkey and sugar cake in the oven
The table set with sweet-burning candles.

But none of it as fragrant to the Father
As the bubbling joy of my soul.

The spilling-over thanksgiving
For dearly-bought salvation

In that musty, hay-filled,
Cross-shadowed manger.

# Songs of Family

# *Prayer for Anna Caroline*

For Anna Caroline Whetstone
January 29, 2001

This child, O Lord,
Whose name means Grace,
We give into Your tender care,
To be surrounded by Your love
And guided by our prayers.

So stir within her heart, we pray,
The gracious notes of praise,
And, Lord, please fill her precious life,
With angels' joyful ways.

*Sing to the Lord a new song, His praise in the assembly of the saints.*

*Psalm 149:1*

# Broken Strings

Sweet broken son, how do I calmly give you up?
How listen, docile, to the words
Of teacher, doctor, counselor,
All trying in their well-trained way
To help you grow—and me to understand?

How can they know how deep into my being
Have gone the tendrils of your self?
How touching my own pain
The hurt etched out in your small frame?
How sweet those growing arms around my heart?

I grasp for you the Dream,
And claw for every foothold,
Up the steep incline of step-and-fall
Holding fast the slipping hope
Of tortured climb toward manhood's goal.

I long to close you up within my arms,
To save you from misunderstanding's taunts,
Protect you in a place where pointed insult
Dares not sling its wrecking stones
And curl you into fetal fear again.

One day, I pray, you'll cherish who you are.
Free then, you'll reach and claim—
And live—that noble Dream,
Then gentled eyes will speak to me of peace,
And understand the love that lets you go.

# Passage

Like a bird caught
In a Snare
I held her close,
She struggled there.

With trembling heart
I let her fly,
Strong, bright-hued wings
Soar wide and high.

# Mama, Where's Daddy Goin'?

"Mama, where's Daddy goin'?"
"To live somewhere else.
You'll see him sometimes."
Confused, guilt-ridden child.

"Mama, where's Daddy goin'?"
"I don't know, Honey.
He's just gone."
Abandoned child.

"Mama, where's Daddy goin'?"
"To prison,
Where he can't hurt you anymore."
Wounded, broken child.

"Mama, where's Daddy goin'?"
"See that cross up there,
Behind the pulpit?
That's where he's goin',
To Heaven, one day."
Blessed child.

# *Song for a Baby Girl*

Addison Hope Whetstone
February 4, 2005

You're such a tiny bundle,
Wrapped in your blanket pink—
We wonder what your eyes can see,
What baby thoughts you think.

Those perfect, tiny hands and feet,
Eyelashes softly curled—
So carefully created
By One who made the world.

Sweet little girl, gift from Above,
Our prayer is that you'll grow
Each day to live in Jesus' love,
Each year His grace to know.

May the God of *Hope* fill you with all joy and peace,
as you trust in Him, so that you may overflow
With *Hope* by the power of the Holy Spirit.
Romans 15:13

# Unclaimed

Her small face haunts my days
Eyes wide and cold
From seeing too much death,
Her smile tentative,
Not quite trusting,
Her need reaching into my heart.

She is the face of
Unwanted girl-children
Sold into slavery of men
Before her baby-soft skin
Has covered filled-out limbs,
Or breasts or hips.

Something precious
Looks out from the deep dark eyes,
A wisp of knowledge buried there,
The lost sense of belovedness,
Someone's protecting arms, a voice,
A passing memory of who she is.

***

Upon her bed, in safety's sleep,
I watch my own beloved child
Whose stardust dreams of love protect,
Assure her future, bright and full
Of joyful opportunity,
To discover daily who she is.

Lord, how Your heart must break
At sight of those whose empty eyes
Speak of abandonment and pain.
They are Your precious children too,
Formed in careful patterns,
Meant to be claimed by Love.

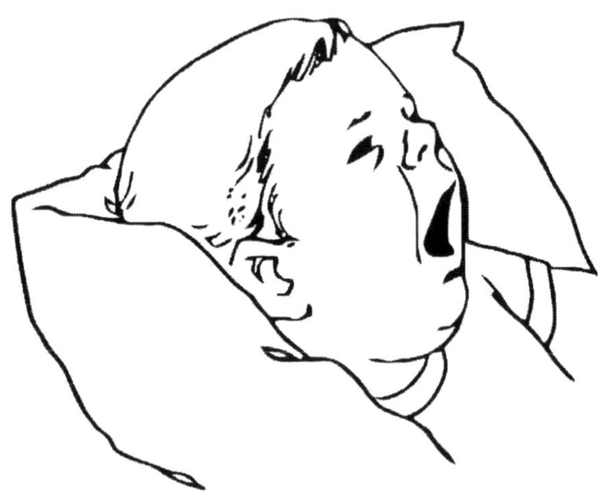

# *Welcome to a Baby Boy*

Edwin Alexander Whetstone
February 27, 1996

Dear little boy, now wrapped in sleep,
Our daily joy, our nightly prayer.
Your brand new life a charge to keep,
With angels hovering everywhere.

Those baby hands and tiny feet
Will soon be busy, finding out,
In ways that sometimes won't be neat,
Just what this world is all about.

And soon we know, you'll learn to walk,
To read and run and ride a bike,
To play computer games—and talk.
Play ball and marbles, camp and hike.

Sweet tiny boy, for whom we pray
May Jesus guide you all the way.

For we are God's workmanship created in Christ Jesus
to do good works, which God prepared in advance for us to do.
Ephesians 2:10

© Schoolplaten.com

# Wonder Song

"It wonders me"--her voice is low—
"What songs the pretty birds all know.

And trees and rainbows, rivers too—
I just can't understand. Can you?"

It wonders me and wraps me 'round,
By faith to see the Word abound.

Creation came by *Let there be* . . .
And You have even molded me.

It wonders me to hear and know
Your Word commands the oceans' flow.

Knee-deep in glory, I rejoice
That Wonder Love has such a Voice.

# Hint of Lavender

Gentle as the April morning
Fragrant, fragile lilacs bloom,
Touch my senses, caress my soul.
The tree you planted.

One long ago sad April morning
A hand-made lavender blouse
Hung on my door, touched my pain.
The grief you shared.

To Julie

# *Prayer for a New Home*

Lord, Jesus, be the Joy and Light
Of this dear couple's home.
Fill with Thy love each day and night
And brighten every room.

In times of stress and times of ease
May they Thy Spirit know,
And always may they seek to please
The Lord Who loves them so.

Be present at their table, Lord
The Host at every meal.
Bless them with hunger for Thy Word,
Thy grace to them reveal.

Lord Jesus, be the Joy and Light
Of this dear couple's home.
Protect them both by Thy great might,
And reign in every room.

# Incense

A mother's prayer of thanksgiving

Such fragrance is here, O my Lord,
To walk with my small ones and talk,
Just after the September rain.

Deep sweetness of fellowship comes
With touching the soft silkened seed
And watching its high, fragile flight.

The scent of bright maple and pine,
The red-berried dogwood that bow
To squishing-up mud by the road.

Delicious, O Lord, as Thy Word
Is this moment of golden-robed day,
To share with young hearts turned to Thee.

# Misty Thoughts

I watch her standing there,
Brave smile securely in place
Before those cold and careless brick buildings,
Alone, among a throng of strangers.

Over and over we were welcomed
To her academic career,
Escorted by warm and weary sophomores
To a bare but tangled room, our daughter's new home.

All her trophies were there—
Worn stuffed animals, books, posters,
Pictures of family and boyfriend.
There dwelt the promise of
A giggling toddler,
A self-conscious schoolgirl,
A confident young lady—
And the merriment of a household.

Did we do any of it right?
Will she remember the good times,
Warm family holidays, triumphant performances,
Sweet, late-night talks, prom dresses and wilted corsages?

Can she forget sibling arguments,
Hard discipline lessons,
Raised voices of parents trying too hard
Because they love so much?

In the car beside her silent father
I remember a squirming infant given
Solemnly and joyfully to God in baptism.

*We're back again, Lord,*
*To turn her over to Your care.*

# Going to High School

Can you believe it?
The summer of swimming
And skating,
And sleeping
And traveling all over
Is gone.

It's time now for lockers
And backpacks too full,
Of half-eaten lunches
And books, lots of books.

Of schedules that frustrate you
Girls that confuse you
And teachers
Who expect 'way too much.

I pray for you daily,
My precious first-grandson,
And ask that your studies
Will capture your thoughts
And your heart—

That this year of growing
Will be the best yet
And you'll search for
And find—in the Very Best Book—
God's great Plan
For the life only He has for you.

# A Prayer As You Graduate

A gift to my first grandson, Christopher Bryant Thomas, at his high school graduation

Before us you stand straight and tall,
The childhood years behind you.
Surrounded now by so much love
And wishes to remind you.

But now it's time to let you go
A kiss through tears, a bended knee
To show our love and send a prayer
Wherever you may grow to be.

We pray for riches—not for gold,
But understanding from Above—
To know the Mystery of God
In Christ, the hidden Source of Love.

In Him is all you need to know,
Whatever claims your heart and mind.
The treasures rich of wisdom's grace
In Jesus Christ the Lord you'll find.

Taken from a prayer of St. Paul, in Colossians 2:2

# Going to a New School

For Jerry Hunter Thomas
September, 2002

There once was a fellow
Whose grandmother thought
He was the sweetest
Boy in the world.

And now he's grown tall,
And he's going to school,
And he's still Grandma's
Sweet little boy.

But you're learning new things,
And working so hard—
And sometimes
You'll just want to stop it and play.

I pray that you'll find it exciting and fun,
And your dear heart will grow every day
To know Jesus' love and His wonderful care
In all that you're learning to do.

# Small Devotion

I bring to You this night, Dear Lord
All those small things that fill my day.

The faucet's small relentless drip,
So like a child's repeated "why?".

The fleeting look of hurt on my son's face
When angry words steal his response.

The small cry of a five-year-old in the night
And the long pull up steep stairs in half-sleep.

The wet pants and mud-spattered dress
As the last load of wash is spinning.

Small fingers needing a constant "no!"
Soft brown eyes pleading with my anger.

Young drawings demanding praise, like
Small tasks—ill-done but proudly so—

Small toys and parts of same,
ALWAYS in my hurried path.

One small room, rumpled host to wandering dolls,
Bits of creativity and a very young woman's finery.

Short arms that reach for one more goodnight
As I kiss sleepy-pillowed heads
and join their prayers to mine.

# The Gunny Sack

A mother's lament

I filled it up with sobs and sighs
Of pain and pity sore.
I named the reasons I'd been hurt,
The rights they'd trampled o'er.

"He robs me of my self-respect,
Their needs are all they see.
I can't go on, it hurts too much—
And no one cares for me."

Then fell across my piteous soul
A rugged-shadowed cross
And deep within my heart a voice,
"All rights—but one—are loss."

Upon my knees I sobbed new pain
My Savior's form to see
And dropped that filthy gunny sack
There at His wounded feet.

The only right I'll ever need
Was blood-bought on a tree.
The royal right—poor as I am—
God's loving child to be.

Weeping may endure for the night, but joy cometh in the morning.

Psalm 30:5

# Anniversary of My Grief

My grief is old
I'm weary of it.
Friends have long forgotten
Some never knew—or cared.

My grief is old
But always new
In lonely midnight hours
And weariness unshared.

My grief is old
Not cutting fresh,
Alarming, every-moment pain,
Yet—where is there release?

My grief is old
Now packed away
A musty-boxed memorial for
Sweet healing prayers—and peace.

# Songs of Devotion

# Darning Thread

When I'm needed the most I'm falling apart.
Like the sweater I'm mending,
All the threads have become frayed
At the points of most wear,
And there is a gaping hole.

The soft lavender of peace is broken harshly,
That yellow joy-yarn thinned to nothing.
The red laughter one's been cut;
Complaining fills the place it used to be.
The cool green of song has shredded
And disappeared.

I cannot gather up these ends again–
They are forever broken–
But the darning thread of Love
Never thins or frays,
Never ravels at the edges.

Oh Lord God, sew me together again,
So that the rubbed-out spot
Where I've been too much used
Can be a strong, safe place
For leaning and holding on.

With the needle of forgiveness and faith
Mend the person I was going to be,
Make me into the mother You planned
In the perfection of Your pattern Book.

# Heart-Shaped Nest

Each sin forgiven,
Each sorrow quenched,
Each day of undeserved
Sweet fellowship.

Like downy feathers
Make soft the nest
For Love, the Son
To live and grow.

# Campfire

Sparks fly upward,
Voices rise in harmony,
Easy laughter,
companionship,
Praise on lifted hands.

Sparks fly upward,
Faces brightened by flames
Marshmallows taste
crisp-sweet
And sooty on my tongue.

Sparks fly upward
Like my sin, inevitable,
irretrievable.
Like my shattered heart,
Lifted heavenward.

Now faith is
the substance
of things hoped
for, the
evidence of
things not
seen.

Hebrews 11:1

# Faith

I cannot understand, my Lord,
How You could wipe away my sin,
And by a gracious, solemn Word
You still the voice of dread within.

How can Your Spirit, shining through,
Work miracles of peace and health,
You bring my saddened soul to You
On golden streams of heaven's wealth.

But I believe that blood was shed,
Upon my dusty, sin-soaked earth,
And, helpless, from a manger-bed
You gazed on Calvary, at birth.

And I can trust Your dying Love,
Stretched there in pain for me.
Unfathomed mercy, grace unbound,
In Resurrection life I see.

# Restoration

At dawn I walked the sparkling beach,
Near-stroked the soft pink gauze of sky,

I watched the sand crabs, skittering, hide
Surf-washed, defenseless, deposited there,

Returned the smile of a burnished child
Who greeted the day with his empty pail,

Laughed at the hungry, long-legged bird
Plucking breakfast from the incandescent foam.

I felt no longer old . . .
stiff . . .
sad . . .
used-up,
Unwanted, or alone.

But clean and open . . .
Rejoicing . . .
Youth-ful,
Over-indulged by Creation-Love.

# Bethany

Lord Jesus, this morning I kneel at Your feet,
Like Mary with spikenard spilled,
Cleaning a bathroom—in service to You—
In a home where the joy has been stilled.

For their sweet child is dying, and taking with her
The brightness and giggles of song,
Her dancing feet limp, her voice a mere whisper,
The promise of womanhood gone.

Like Martha, whose busy hands worshiped You, Lord
I come with my sponge and my gloves,
To kneel here in prayer, and pour out for them.
The unquenchable scent of Your Love.

Written on Saturday, May 18, 2002

# *Bottled*

Put my tears in Thy bottle
Psalm 65:8 (KJV)

Safely in Your keeping, Lord
The grief of a year is put away.
And memories—even the sad ones—
Are eased, without pain,
Each sealed in its own fragrance.

You've been here, too, Lord
In the searing time of giving up,
The empty anger that a child is gone,
The sweetness of holding small things
And wrapping them away.

Now the time for tears is past,
You never said there shouldn't be any.
You only said You have a place for them.
Gracious Lord, only unthinkable love
Could cherish my grief, and refine it to joy.

# Call Me Mara

Based on Ruth 1:20-21

Echo from the distant hills
Music without sound
Sorrow looking for a place
Loneliness unbound
Call me Mara*

Sprinkled tears upon the night
Light of peace now dimmed
Wanderer of silent rooms
Eyes with sadness rimmed
Call me Mara

Searching spirit feeling forth
Reaching up in vain
Stumbling, falling, burdened down
Prisoner to pain
Call me Mara

Blinking, groping for the light
Pushing past the pain
Find a steady, loving Hand
Learn to sing again
Call me Naomi**

**Bitter* ***Pleasant*

# Evensong

A Visit to St. Giles Cathedral. Edinburgh, Scotland

Alone I walk on foreign streets,
And climb the worn cathedral steps
Into another century,
Absorbed at once in reverent solitude.

Stone vaulted arches
Darkened by smoke of a million candles
Echo long remembered sounds—
Chanting choirs, splendid-robed and solemn,
One fiery preacher
Changing history from the ornate pulpit-box.

Tall, sun-streamed windows crafted millennia ago
Portray a Savior with children on His knee,
Calvary's sin-bought pain,
Wondrous Easter,
Angel-attended ascension,
The Holy Word adorned with light and color.

In a small side chapel I kneel to worship
With unseen ancestors of kin and confession.
I weep for faith remembered,
Blood shed for this freedom.

Outside on darkening streets,
I am no longer alone,
A foreigner in a strange land.
I claim a heritage of faith
At Evensong.

# Invitation to Pain

What do you suppose the Almighty was thinking,
When ancient in heaven He sat.
At the end of five days—
Or five aeons—whatever the span of His week,
He viewed His perfection of creature and plant,
And decided He needed . . .
A man?

Yet stranger than that one, or so it says here,
He wanted a woman, anon,
To finish, to round out, give meaning and joy,
To the whole whirling, light-faceted sphere
Of beginning, bewildering life.
And took, it states plainly,
A bone from the man, to make someone
Helpful to him.

But helpful she wasn't
And you and I know that without
All their troublesome pranks,
God might have gone blissfully, thousands of aeons
Creating wild things in obedient communion with Him.

Yet, would He have missed, down some mystical age,
The agonized pleasure of hearing
From one whom He loved
A sobbing, "O Father, I'm sorry.
Please make me a way to come Home."

And would He have fashioned Golgotha,
Without any reason to be?

# Psalm 8

*O Lord . . . Our Lord, How majestic is Thy Name*
*In all the earth.*

This morning, lost in Majesty,
I wonder at the grace that
Gives me permission to call Thee
*My* Lord.

Watching Thee pull life-giving sun
From a saffron sea,
Cover it with clouds,
Sweep the broad sky with soft-rayed light.

I am prostrated by humility,
Burst open with outlandish praise,
Soaring into
Eternities of Joy.

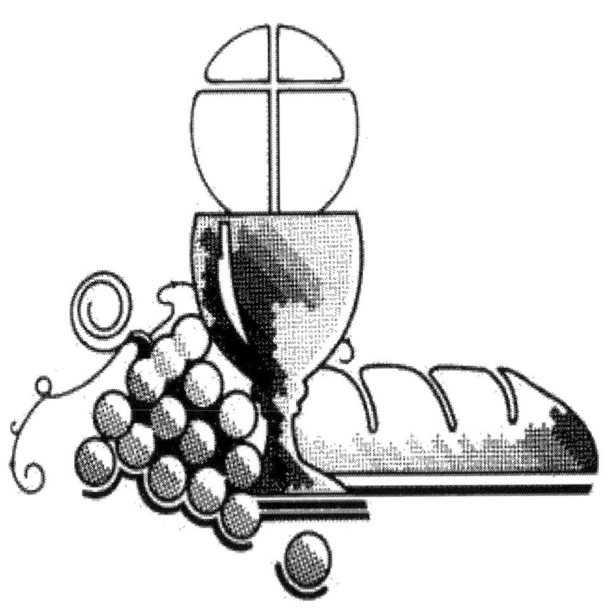

# Sacrament

Are they clean?
A man's hands break the loaf
And pour out wine for me.
Irreverently I wonder
About sanitation.

Jesus, Lord, forgive!
My own hands are too soiled
To take these elements
Which signify Your
Suffering for my soul.

I don't like suffering.
What I enjoy are songs of victory,
Triumph,
Praise and Adoration.
Not wounded side,
Bloody tears,
Stretched-out agony.

But there is no victory without that pain,
No triumph 'til You conquered death,
And praise discovers all that Love—
Who bids me share communion loaf and cup—
Has won, through agony, for me.

I am on my face in adoration.

"When I awake, I am still with Thee."
Psalm 139:18 (KJV)

The morning came softly,
Slipping on apologetic tiptoe,
After the night's
Wet, lashing fury.

Urged by waking birds,
The dawn-light grew and burst
On damp, despondent earth
Its sparkling day.

# The Visit

What is man, that Thou visitest him?
Psalm 8 (KJV)

High on a hilltop—the night is clear—
I gaze entranced as stars appear.

First, "wish I may and wish I might,"
Then Pleiades, the Dippers, Orion, alight.

A universe I can't perceive
Lies past the sparkled evening sea.

A mighty Hand is holding all
I bow to Majesty in thrall.

# *Niagara*

The thunder falls go on and on,
The mist rises into sunshine, rainbow arches—
Promises,
Fades
And dies.

The power untamed, life-taking, mesmerizing
Ancients worshipped here, amazed, afraid
Of gods below
The thunder
Power.

So too I bow before the God of Promises
Whose thunderous Voice calls to me
I hear
And know
And worship.

The sound of many waters echoes through the mist
Unaltered beauty, unending, terrifying roar
Holiness
Eternal
Sound

My heart is bowed before the blinding white.
Omnipotent majesty unleashed in time
Crystal creation
Awesome
Love.

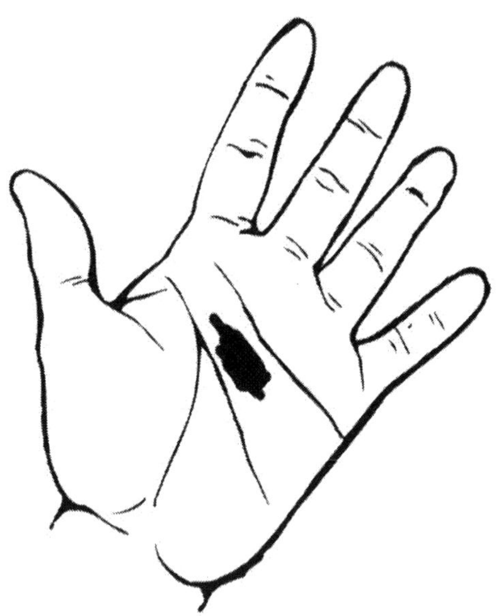

# The Palm of His Hand

I have graven you on the palm of my hand.
Isaiah 49:16

In the palm of His hand are the scars of my sin
The ugly, dark, deep holes that I see
From nails driven deeply and sharply within,
Oh how Jesus suffered for me!

The palm of His hand holds the essence of me
The mercy that took all the horror of sin
Engraved for the Father in heaven to see,
A child now redeemed, claiming kin.

On the palm of His hand is engraven my name,
Forever the story is written above
Whatever of sorrow, or hatred or blame
The whole is now covered with love.

# Nonsense Songs

# Samuel's Salamander's Lament

Lord, I was just lying there in the sun.
It felt so good after the slime of the creek bed.

Where is there a place so soft and solid
As years of leaves on the forest floor?

I know You made me to slink along,
Careful of big feet and small inquisitive hands.

I do trust Your protection, Lord,
My brown-green coloring, so like my habitat.

But, oh, if I could—just once—
Stay long enough in the sun to soak its warmth,

Without fear of shriveling to nothing
Before I can slide back home.

# Cobwebbed

The back of my mind is a rumbling caboose
Attached to the train of my day.
With so little order, and even less use
It's a box labeled "stash this away."

The back of my mind is a fairyland place
Where *Somedays* are dancing around,
The fanciful idols of grammar and grace,
Of wishing and dreaming abound.

But the back of my mind has some solid old shelves,
Of stories and characters dear
I'll give to them life—in spite of themselves—
And publish a poem, right here!

# Mother's Window

All the oak leaves are brown now,
Hovering
Against the coming chill.
The scarlet bird comes to feed
At the barren maple's box.

Sunlight slides under ruffled panels,
Across purple winter violets
And spills on the round red rug,
Where the cat curls,
And licks,
And settles to sleep.

I am surrounded by quiet
Until the school bus comes.

# Mournful Lament for Monday

The trash cans all are full today,
And drooping on the floor
Are sodden mounds of towels piled
Against the bathroom door.

There's Sunday's great and funny news,
Half-emptied cups that lurk
Beneath the chairs that mark my path
To hours of clean-up work.

This solemn, empty day reflects
A weekend's recklessness,
And all my pride in motherhood
Is raving helplessness.

But sogginess and stickiness,
Like pieces of my heart,
Can all be set aright again
With loving, patient art.

For this wrecked place is home, and so—
For all the mess they bring—
I give my thanks and praise to God
For each teenager's *thing*.

*ISTJ* - *The Duty Fulfillers*
*ESTJ* - *The Guardians*
*ISFJ* - *The Nurturers*
*ESFJ* - *The Caregivers*
*ISTP* - *The Mechanics*
*ESTP* - *The Doers*
*ESFP* - *The Performers*
*ISFP* - *The Artists*
*ENTJ* - *The Executives*
*INTJ* - *The Scientists*
*ENTP* - *The Visionaries*
*INTP* - *The Thinkers*
*ENFJ* - *The Givers*
*INFJ* - *The Protectors*
*ENFP* - *The Inspirers*
*INFP* - *The Idealists*

# *Plotted Personality*

Thoughts on Personality Profile Testing

How wonderful to know for sure
Just who I am–
Or who I think I am—
Or seem to others I might be,
Because of all that I appear to be.

With every square correctly filled,
We know just how I will react
To any given stimuli.
As, classified and categorized,
My tendencies are graphed in place,
Describing in a solemn phrase
The intimate inside of me.

But You were there when I was made
From ancient chromosome design
In secret, complicated space.
Before You set a universe to whirl,
Or hollowed out the seas,
Or planted palms and cedars forth
Where one day ambling giants would kneel
To worship by a stone.

Does it even matter then,
My tendencied behavior?
When You've been sure—forever now—
Of how my psych and self would grow,
And, looking once at Calvary's love,
Respond with unplanned tears of joy,
To know my God's creative touch.

Made in the USA
Columbia, SC
22 June 2020

10622917R00072